Plan the Podcast of Your Dreams

This Planner Belongs To

_____

Welcome to the Spark Media Podcast Planner!

Hi! I'm Misty Phillip, the host of the By His Grace Podcast and founder of Spark Media. As I was planning the inaugural Spark event, I got the Spark Podcast Planner idea, a resource I wish I would have had when I began podcasting. Our first planner was made specifically for 2020. Since then, we have made modifications and updates to the Spark Planner to allow you to use it anytime.

This updated planner is designed to help you create, market, and launch the podcast of your dreams. Once you establish your podcast, you will have a place to create your goals, brainstorm podcast ideas, evaluate your episodes, track podcast growth, and capture all of your fantastic podcasting ideas.

Before you launch your podcast, let's cast a vision for what you would like your podcast to be. There is a series of vision casting and goal setting worksheets, including checklists of to-do's before you pick up your mic and once your episode is live. It also includes a month at a glance to write in all of the important dates for the month.

Vision

One Year Goals

Potential Guests

Potential Sponsors

Collaboration Ideas

Before You Pick Up The Mic

Branding

Podcast Checklist

Episode Planning Pages

Once Your Podcast is Live

The Spark Planner helps you to create a podcasting workflow and organize all your ideas.

Happy Planning,

Misty Phillip

Commit your work to the LORD, and your plans will be established

- Proverbs 16:3

Before You Pick Up the Mic

What type of show?

- ☐ Solo
- ☐ Co-Host
- ☐ Interview
- ☐ Storytelling

How long will your podcast be?

- ☐ 5-15 minutes
- ☐ 15-30 minutes
- ☐ 30-60 minutes
- ☐ Over an hour

Purpose: Inspire, Educate or Entertain

What does your listener struggle with?

How can your podcast help them?

What are their pain-points?

How can you serve your listener?

How frequently will you release a show?

- ☐ Daily
- ☐ 2-3 episodes a week
- ☐ 1 episode a week
- ☐ 2 episodes a month

Ideal listener?

- ☐ Who is your ideal listener?
- ☐ Men, Women or Both
- ☐ Age range
- ☐ Likes
- ☐ Dislikes

Branding

Think through your podcast brand and aesthetic

- How do you want people to feel when they listen to your show?

- How do you want them to respond when they encounter your brand?

COLORS

COLOR NAME   COLOR NAME   COLOR NAME

FONTS   **TAGLINE**

HEADLINES: FONT NAME

                                                    GRAPHIC ELEMENTS/ICONS

BODY COPY: FONT NAME

PRIMARY LOGO

                                                    PATTERNS/TEXTURES

Podcast Checklist

- [ ] Podcast Name

  _____

  _____

  _____

- [ ] Tag line

  _____

  _____

  _____

- [ ] Podcast Description

  _____

  _____

  _____

- [ ] Podcast Artwork

  _____

  _____

  _____

- [ ] USB Microphone

  _____

  _____

  _____

- [ ] Audio Editing Software

  _____

  _____

  _____

- [ ] Website Domain Name

  _____

  _____

  _____

- [ ] Podcast Hosting

  _____

  _____

One Year Podcast

In three months my podcast will:

In six months my podcast will:

In twelve months my podcast will:

Goals

_____

_____

_____

_____

_____

_____

_____

_____

_____

_____

_____

_____

_____

_____

Potential Guests

Date	Name	Contact	Response

Potential Guests

Date	Name	Contact	Response

Potential Sponsors

Date   Name   Contact   Response

_____

_____

_____

_____

_____

_____

_____

_____

_____

_____

_____

_____

_____

_____

Collaboration Ideas

Calendar

MON	TUE	WED	THU	FRI	SAT	SUN

TO DO'S

- ☐
- ☐
- ☐
- ☐
- ☐
- ☐
- ☐
- ☐
- ☐
- ☐
- ☐

NOTES

Monthly Goals

_____

_____

_____

_____

_____

_____

_____

_____

_____

_____

_____

_____

_____

_____

Calendar

MON	TUE	WED	THU	FRI	SAT	SUN

TO DO'S

- [ ]
- [ ]
- [ ]
- [ ]
- [ ]
- [ ]
- [ ]
- [ ]
- [ ]
- [ ]
- [ ]

NOTES

Monthly Goals

_____

_____

_____

_____

_____

_____

_____

_____

_____

_____

_____

_____

_____

_____

Calendar

MON	TUE	WED	THU	FRI	SAT	SUN

TO DO'S

- [ ]
- [ ]
- [ ]
- [ ]
- [ ]
- [ ]
- [ ]
- [ ]
- [ ]
- [ ]
- [ ]

NOTES

Monthly Goals

Calendar

MON	TUE	WED	THU	FRI	SAT	SUN

TO DO'S

- [ ]
- [ ]
- [ ]
- [ ]
- [ ]
- [ ]
- [ ]
- [ ]
- [ ]
- [ ]
- [ ]

NOTES

Monthly Goals

_____

_____

_____

_____

_____

_____

_____

_____

_____

_____

_____

_____

_____

_____

Calendar

MON	TUE	WED	THU	FRI	SAT	SUN

TO DO'S

- ☐
- ☐
- ☐
- ☐
- ☐
- ☐
- ☐
- ☐
- ☐
- ☐
- ☐

NOTES

Monthly Goals

Calendar

MON	TUE	WED	THU	FRI	SAT	SUN

TO DO'S

- [ ]
- [ ]
- [ ]
- [ ]
- [ ]
- [ ]
- [ ]
- [ ]
- [ ]
- [ ]
- [ ]

NOTES

Monthly Goals

_____

_____

_____

_____

_____

_____

_____

_____

_____

_____

_____

_____

_____

_____

Calendar

MON	TUE	WED	THU	FRI	SAT	SUN

TO DO'S

- ☐
- ☐
- ☐
- ☐
- ☐
- ☐
- ☐
- ☐
- ☐
- ☐
- ☐

NOTES

Monthly Goals

_____

_____

_____

_____

_____

_____

_____

_____

_____

_____

_____

_____

_____

Calendar

MON	TUE	WED	THU	FRI	SAT	SUN

TO DO'S

- [ ]
- [ ]
- [ ]
- [ ]
- [ ]
- [ ]
- [ ]
- [ ]
- [ ]
- [ ]
- [ ]

NOTES

Monthly Goals

_____

_____

_____

_____

_____

_____

_____

_____

_____

_____

_____

_____

_____

_____

Calendar

MON	TUE	WED	THU	FRI	SAT	SUN

TO DO'S

- ☐
- ☐
- ☐
- ☐
- ☐
- ☐
- ☐
- ☐
- ☐
- ☐
- ☐

NOTES

Monthly Goals

_____

_____

_____

_____

_____

_____

_____

_____

_____

_____

_____

_____

_____

Calendar

MON	TUE	WED	THU	FRI	SAT	SUN

TO DO'S

☐ _____
☐ _____
☐ _____
☐ _____
☐ _____
☐ _____
☐ _____
☐ _____
☐ _____
☐ _____
☐

NOTES

Monthly Goals

_____

_____

_____

_____

_____

_____

_____

_____

_____

_____

_____

_____

_____

_____

Calendar

MON	TUE	WED	THU	FRI	SAT	SUN

TO DO'S

- [ ]
- [ ]
- [ ]
- [ ]
- [ ]
- [ ]
- [ ]
- [ ]
- [ ]
- [ ]
- [ ]

NOTES

Monthly Goals

_____

_____

_____

_____

_____

_____

_____

_____

_____

_____

_____

_____

_____

Calendar

MON	TUE	WED	THU	FRI	SAT	SUN

TO DO'S

- [ ]
- [ ]
- [ ]
- [ ]
- [ ]
- [ ]
- [ ]
- [ ]
- [ ]
- [ ]
- [ ]

NOTES

Monthly Goals

Episode Planner

PURPOSE: INSPIRE / EDUCATE / ENTERTAIN

BIO:

_____

_____

_____

_____

_____

_____

_____

_____

_____

_____

_____

Title

_____

Topic

_____

_____

_____

Guest

CONTACT:

_____

_____

WEBSITE:

_____

_____

SOCIAL MEDIA:

_____

_____

MAIN POINTS / QUESTIONS TO ASK

- _____
- _____
- _____

CALL TO ACTION

_____

_____

_____

_____

Episode Details

TITLE: _____

GUEST: _____   RECORDING DATE: _____

TOPIC: _____   PUBLISHED DATE: _____

EPISODE #: _____

EP LENGTH: _____

RECORDING LIST

- [ ] _____
- [ ] _____
- [ ] _____
- [ ] _____
- [ ] _____
- [ ] _____
- [ ] _____

EDITING LIST

- [ ] _____
- [ ] _____
- [ ] _____
- [ ] _____
- [ ] _____
- [ ] _____
- [ ] _____

PUBLISHING LIST

- [ ] _____
- [ ] _____
- [ ] _____
- [ ] _____
- [ ] _____
- [ ] _____
- [ ] _____

INTRO

_____
_____
_____

IDEAS / INTERVIEW QUESTIONS

_____
_____
_____
_____
_____
_____
_____
_____
_____
_____
_____
_____
_____
_____
_____
_____

SHOW NOTES

_____
_____
_____
_____
_____
_____
_____
_____
_____
_____
_____
_____
_____

OUTRO

_____
_____
_____

Episode Planner

BIO:

_____

Title

CONTACT:

_____

_____

Topic

_____
_____
_____

WEBSITE:

_____

_____

SOCIAL MEDIA:

_____

_____

Guest

MAIN POINTS / QUESTIONS TO ASK

- _____
- _____
- _____

CALL TO ACTION

_____
_____
_____

Episode Details

TITLE: _____

GUEST: _____

TOPIC: _____

RECORDING DATE: _____

PUBLISHED DATE: _____

EPISODE #: _____

EP LENGTH: _____

RECORDING LIST

☐ _____
☐ _____
☐ _____
☐ _____
☐ _____
☐ _____
☐ _____

INTRO

_____
_____
_____

IDEAS / INTERVIEW QUESTIONS

_____
_____
_____
_____
_____
_____
_____
_____
_____
_____
_____
_____
_____
_____
_____
_____

EDITING LIST

☐ _____
☐ _____
☐ _____
☐ _____
☐ _____
☐ _____
☐ _____

SHOW NOTES

_____
_____
_____
_____
_____
_____
_____
_____
_____
_____
_____
_____

PUBLISHING LIST

☐ _____
☐ _____
☐ _____
☐ _____
☐ _____
☐ _____
☐ _____

OUTRO

_____
_____
_____

Episode Planner

PURPOSE: INSPIRE / EDUCATE / ENTERTAIN

BIO:

Title

CONTACT:

Topic

WEBSITE:

SOCIAL MEDIA:

Guest

MAIN POINTS / QUESTIONS TO ASK

- _____
- _____
- _____

CALL TO ACTION

Episode Details

TITLE: _____

GUEST: _____   RECORDING DATE: _____

TOPIC: _____   PUBLISHED DATE: _____

_____   EPISODE #: _____

EP LENGTH: _____

RECORDING LIST

- [ ] _____
- [ ] _____
- [ ] _____
- [ ] _____
- [ ] _____
- [ ] _____
- [ ] _____

EDITING LIST

- [ ] _____
- [ ] _____
- [ ] _____
- [ ] _____
- [ ] _____
- [ ] _____
- [ ] _____

PUBLISHING LIST

- [ ] _____
- [ ] _____
- [ ] _____
- [ ] _____
- [ ] _____
- [ ] _____
- [ ] _____

INTRO

_____
_____
_____

IDEAS / INTERVIEW QUESTIONS

_____
_____
_____
_____
_____
_____
_____
_____
_____
_____
_____
_____
_____
_____
_____

SHOW NOTES

_____
_____
_____
_____
_____
_____
_____
_____
_____
_____
_____

OUTRO

_____
_____
_____

Episode Planner

BIO:

_____

Title

_____
_____
_____
_____
_____
_____
_____
_____
_____
_____

CONTACT:

_____
_____
_____

Topic

_____
_____
_____

WEBSITE:

_____
_____
_____

SOCIAL MEDIA:

_____
_____
_____

Guest

MAIN POINTS / QUESTIONS TO ASK

- _____
- _____
- _____

CALL TO ACTION

_____
_____
_____
_____
_____

Episode Details

TITLE: _____

GUEST: _____   RECORDING DATE: _____

TOPIC: _____   PUBLISHED DATE: _____

_____   EPISODE #: _____

EP LENGTH: _____

RECORDING LIST

- ☐ _____
- ☐ _____
- ☐ _____
- ☐ _____
- ☐ _____
- ☐ _____
- ☐ _____

INTRO

_____
_____
_____

IDEAS / INTERVIEW QUESTIONS

_____
_____
_____
_____
_____
_____
_____
_____
_____
_____
_____
_____
_____
_____
_____

EDITING LIST

- ☐ _____
- ☐ _____
- ☐ _____
- ☐ _____
- ☐ _____
- ☐ _____
- ☐ _____

PUBLISHING LIST

- ☐ _____
- ☐ _____
- ☐ _____
- ☐ _____
- ☐ _____
- ☐ _____
- ☐ _____

SHOW NOTES

_____
_____
_____
_____
_____
_____
_____
_____
_____
_____
_____
_____
_____

OUTRO

_____
_____
_____

Episode Planner

BIO:
_____

Title

CONTACT:
_____

Topic
_____
_____
_____

WEBSITE:
_____

SOCIAL MEDIA:
_____

Guest

MAIN POINTS / QUESTIONS TO ASK

- _____
- _____
- _____

CALL TO ACTION

_____
_____
_____
_____
_____

Episode Details

TITLE: _____

GUEST: _____

RECORDING DATE: _____

PUBLISHED DATE: _____

TOPIC: _____

EPISODE #: _____

EP LENGTH: _____

RECORDING LIST

☐ _____
☐ _____
☐ _____
☐ _____
☐ _____
☐ _____
☐ _____

INTRO

_____
_____
_____

IDEAS / INTERVIEW QUESTIONS

_____
_____
_____
_____
_____
_____
_____
_____
_____
_____
_____
_____
_____
_____
_____
_____
_____

EDITING LIST

☐ _____
☐ _____
☐ _____
☐ _____
☐ _____
☐ _____
☐ _____

PUBLISHING LIST

☐ _____
☐ _____
☐ _____
☐ _____
☐ _____
☐ _____
☐ _____

SHOW NOTES

_____
_____
_____
_____
_____
_____
_____
_____
_____
_____
_____
_____

OUTRO

_____
_____
_____

Episode Planner

BIO:

_____
Title

CONTACT:
_____
_____
_____

_____
_____
_____
_____
_____

Topic
_____
_____
_____

WEBSITE:
_____
_____

_____
_____
_____
_____
_____
_____

SOCIAL MEDIA:
_____
_____

_____
Guest

MAIN POINTS / QUESTIONS TO ASK

- _____
- _____
- _____

CALL TO ACTION

_____
_____
_____
_____
_____

Episode Details

TITLE: _____

GUEST: _____

TOPIC: _____

RECORDING DATE: _____

PUBLISHED DATE: _____

EPISODE #: _____

EP LENGTH: _____

RECORDING LIST

- [ ] _____
- [ ] _____
- [ ] _____
- [ ] _____
- [ ] _____
- [ ] _____
- [ ] _____

EDITING LIST

- [ ] _____
- [ ] _____
- [ ] _____
- [ ] _____
- [ ] _____
- [ ] _____
- [ ] _____

PUBLISHING LIST

- [ ] _____
- [ ] _____
- [ ] _____
- [ ] _____
- [ ] _____
- [ ] _____
- [ ] _____

INTRO

_____
_____
_____

IDEAS / INTERVIEW QUESTIONS

_____
_____
_____
_____
_____
_____
_____
_____
_____
_____
_____
_____
_____
_____
_____
_____
_____

SHOW NOTES

_____
_____
_____
_____
_____
_____
_____
_____
_____
_____
_____

OUTRO

_____
_____
_____

Episode Planner

BIO:

Title

CONTACT:

Topic

WEBSITE:

SOCIAL MEDIA:

Guest

MAIN POINTS / QUESTIONS TO ASK

- _____
- _____
- _____

CALL TO ACTION

Episode Details

TITLE: _____

GUEST: _____

TOPIC: _____

RECORDING DATE: _____

PUBLISHED DATE: _____

EPISODE #: _____

EP LENGTH: _____

RECORDING LIST

- ☐ _____
- ☐ _____
- ☐ _____
- ☐ _____
- ☐ _____
- ☐ _____
- ☐ _____

EDITING LIST

- ☐ _____
- ☐ _____
- ☐ _____
- ☐ _____
- ☐ _____
- ☐ _____
- ☐ _____

PUBLISHING LIST

- ☐ _____
- ☐ _____
- ☐ _____
- ☐ _____
- ☐ _____
- ☐ _____
- ☐ _____

INTRO

_____

_____

_____

IDEAS / INTERVIEW QUESTIONS

_____

_____

_____

_____

_____

_____

_____

_____

_____

_____

_____

_____

_____

_____

_____

SHOW NOTES

_____

_____

_____

_____

_____

_____

_____

_____

_____

_____

_____

_____

_____

_____

OUTRO

_____

_____

_____

Episode Planner

BIO:
_____
_____
_____
_____
_____
_____
_____
_____
_____
_____
_____
_____

_____
Title

Topic
_____
_____
_____

Guest

CONTACT:
_____
_____

WEBSITE:
_____
_____

SOCIAL MEDIA:
_____
_____

MAIN POINTS / QUESTIONS TO ASK

- _____
- _____
- _____

CALL TO ACTION

_____
_____
_____
_____

Episode Details

TITLE: _____   RECORDING DATE: _____

GUEST: _____   PUBLISHED DATE: _____

TOPIC: _____   EPISODE #: _____

_____   EP LENGTH: _____

RECORDING LIST

- ☐ _____
- ☐ _____
- ☐ _____
- ☐ _____
- ☐ _____
- ☐ _____
- ☐ _____

EDITING LIST

- ☐ _____
- ☐ _____
- ☐ _____
- ☐ _____
- ☐ _____
- ☐ _____
- ☐ _____

PUBLISHING LIST

- ☐ _____
- ☐ _____
- ☐ _____
- ☐ _____
- ☐ _____
- ☐ _____
- ☐ _____

INTRO

_____

_____

_____

IDEAS / INTERVIEW QUESTIONS

_____

_____

_____

_____

_____

_____

_____

_____

_____

_____

_____

_____

_____

_____

_____

_____

SHOW NOTES

_____

_____

_____

_____

_____

_____

_____

_____

_____

_____

_____

_____

OUTRO

_____

_____

_____

Episode Planner

BIO:
_____
_____
_____
_____
_____
_____
_____
_____
_____
_____
_____

_____
Title

Topic
_____
_____
_____

_____
Guest

CONTACT:
_____
_____

WEBSITE:
_____
_____

SOCIAL MEDIA:
_____
_____

MAIN POINTS / QUESTIONS TO ASK

- _____
- _____
- _____

CALL TO ACTION

_____
_____
_____
_____
_____
_____

Episode Details

TITLE: _____   RECORDING DATE: _____

GUEST: _____   PUBLISHED DATE: _____

TOPIC: _____   EPISODE #: _____

_____   EP LENGTH: _____

RECORDING LIST

☐ _____
☐ _____
☐ _____
☐ _____
☐ _____
☐ _____
☐ _____

EDITING LIST

☐ _____
☐ _____
☐ _____
☐ _____
☐ _____
☐ _____
☐ _____

PUBLISHING LIST

☐ _____
☐ _____
☐ _____
☐ _____
☐ _____
☐ _____
☐ _____

INTRO

_____
_____
_____

IDEAS / INTERVIEW QUESTIONS

_____
_____
_____
_____
_____
_____
_____
_____
_____
_____
_____
_____
_____
_____

SHOW NOTES

_____
_____
_____
_____
_____
_____
_____
_____
_____
_____
_____
_____

OUTRO

_____
_____
_____

Episode Planner

BIO:

_____
_____
_____
_____
_____
_____
_____
_____
_____
_____
_____

_____
Title

Topic
_____
_____
_____

_____
Guest

CONTACT:

_____
_____
_____

WEBSITE:

_____
_____

SOCIAL MEDIA:

_____
_____
_____

MAIN POINTS / QUESTIONS TO ASK

- _____
- _____
- _____

CALL TO ACTION

_____
_____
_____
_____
_____
_____

Episode Details

TITLE: _____

GUEST: _____

TOPIC: _____

RECORDING DATE: _____

PUBLISHED DATE: _____

EPISODE #: _____

EP LENGTH: _____

RECORDING LIST

☐ _____
☐ _____
☐ _____
☐ _____
☐ _____
☐ _____
☐ _____

EDITING LIST

☐ _____
☐ _____
☐ _____
☐ _____
☐ _____
☐ _____
☐ _____

PUBLISHING LIST

☐ _____
☐ _____
☐ _____
☐ _____
☐ _____
☐ _____
☐ _____

INTRO

_____
_____
_____

IDEAS / INTERVIEW QUESTIONS

_____
_____
_____
_____
_____
_____
_____
_____
_____
_____
_____
_____
_____
_____
_____
_____

SHOW NOTES

_____
_____
_____
_____
_____
_____
_____
_____
_____
_____
_____

OUTRO

_____
_____

Episode Planner

PURPOSE: INSPIRE / EDUCATE / ENTERTAIN

BIO:

_____

Title

CONTACT:

Topic

_____

_____

_____

WEBSITE:

SOCIAL MEDIA:

Guest

MAIN POINTS / QUESTIONS TO ASK

- _____
- _____
- _____

CALL TO ACTION

Episode Details

TITLE: _____

GUEST: _____

TOPIC: _____

RECORDING DATE: _____

PUBLISHED DATE: _____

EPISODE #: _____

EP LENGTH: _____

RECORDING LIST

- ☐ _____
- ☐ _____
- ☐ _____
- ☐ _____
- ☐ _____
- ☐ _____
- ☐ _____

EDITING LIST

- ☐ _____
- ☐ _____
- ☐ _____
- ☐ _____
- ☐ _____
- ☐ _____
- ☐ _____

PUBLISHING LIST

- ☐ _____
- ☐ _____
- ☐ _____
- ☐ _____
- ☐ _____
- ☐ _____
- ☐ _____

INTRO

_____
_____
_____

IDEAS / INTERVIEW QUESTIONS

_____
_____
_____
_____
_____
_____
_____
_____
_____
_____
_____
_____
_____
_____
_____
_____
_____
_____

SHOW NOTES

_____
_____
_____
_____
_____
_____
_____
_____
_____
_____
_____
_____
_____
_____

OUTRO

_____
_____
_____

Episode Planner

BIO:

_____
_____
_____
_____
_____
_____
_____
_____
_____
_____
_____
_____

CONTACT:

_____
_____

WEBSITE:

_____
_____

SOCIAL MEDIA:

_____
_____
_____

Title

_____

Topic

_____
_____
_____

Guest

_____

MAIN POINTS / QUESTIONS TO ASK

- _____
- _____
- _____

CALL TO ACTION

_____
_____
_____
_____
_____

Episode Details

TITLE: _____ RECORDING DATE: _____
GUEST: _____ PUBLISHED DATE: _____
TOPIC: _____ EPISODE #: _____
_____ EP LENGTH: _____

RECORDING LIST

☐ _____
☐ _____
☐ _____
☐ _____
☐ _____
☐ _____
☐ _____

INTRO

_____
_____

IDEAS / INTERVIEW QUESTIONS

_____
_____
_____
_____
_____
_____
_____
_____
_____
_____
_____
_____
_____
_____

EDITING LIST

☐ _____
☐ _____
☐ _____
☐ _____
☐ _____
☐ _____
☐ _____

SHOW NOTES

_____
_____
_____
_____
_____
_____
_____
_____
_____
_____
_____
_____

PUBLISHING LIST

☐ _____
☐ _____
☐ _____
☐ _____
☐ _____
☐ _____
☐ _____

OUTRO

_____
_____
_____

Episode Planner

PURPOSE: INSPIRE / EDUCATE / ENTERTAIN

BIO:
_____
_____
_____
_____
_____
_____
_____
_____
_____
_____
_____

_____
Title

Topic
_____
_____
_____

Guest

CONTACT:
_____
_____

WEBSITE:
_____
_____

SOCIAL MEDIA:
_____
_____

MAIN POINTS / QUESTIONS TO ASK

- _____
- _____
- _____

CALL TO ACTION

_____
_____
_____
_____
_____
_____

Episode Details

TITLE: _____   RECORDING DATE: _____

GUEST: _____   PUBLISHED DATE: _____

TOPIC: _____   EPISODE #: _____

_____   EP LENGTH: _____

RECORDING LIST

- ☐ _____
- ☐ _____
- ☐ _____
- ☐ _____
- ☐ _____
- ☐ _____
- ☐ _____

EDITING LIST

- ☐ _____
- ☐ _____
- ☐ _____
- ☐ _____
- ☐ _____
- ☐ _____
- ☐ _____

PUBLISHING LIST

- ☐ _____
- ☐ _____
- ☐ _____
- ☐ _____
- ☐ _____
- ☐ _____
- ☐ _____

INTRO

_____
_____

IDEAS / INTERVIEW QUESTIONS

_____
_____
_____
_____
_____
_____
_____
_____
_____
_____
_____
_____
_____
_____
_____

SHOW NOTES

_____
_____
_____
_____
_____
_____
_____
_____
_____
_____
_____
_____
_____

OUTRO

_____
_____

Episode Planner

BIO:
_____
_____
_____
_____
_____
_____
_____
_____
_____
_____
_____

_____
Title

Topic
_____
_____
_____

_____
Guest

CONTACT:
_____
_____
_____

WEBSITE:
_____

SOCIAL MEDIA:
_____
_____

MAIN POINTS / QUESTIONS TO ASK

• _____
• _____
• _____

CALL TO ACTION

_____
_____
_____
_____
_____
_____

Episode Details

TITLE: _____   RECORDING DATE: _____

GUEST: _____   PUBLISHED DATE: _____

TOPIC: _____   EPISODE #: _____

EP LENGTH: _____

RECORDING LIST

- [ ] _____
- [ ] _____
- [ ] _____
- [ ] _____
- [ ] _____
- [ ] _____
- [ ] _____

EDITING LIST

- [ ] _____
- [ ] _____
- [ ] _____
- [ ] _____
- [ ] _____
- [ ] _____
- [ ] _____

PUBLISHING LIST

- [ ] _____
- [ ] _____
- [ ] _____
- [ ] _____
- [ ] _____
- [ ] _____
- [ ] _____

INTRO

_____
_____
_____

IDEAS / INTERVIEW QUESTIONS

_____
_____
_____
_____
_____
_____
_____
_____
_____
_____
_____
_____
_____
_____
_____
_____
_____

SHOW NOTES

_____
_____
_____
_____
_____
_____
_____
_____
_____
_____
_____
_____

OUTRO

_____
_____

Episode Planner

BIO: _____

_____

_____

_____

_____

_____

_____

_____

_____

_____

_____

_____

_____

Title

Topic

_____

_____

_____

Guest

CONTACT:

_____

_____

_____

WEBSITE:

_____

_____

SOCIAL MEDIA:

_____

_____

_____

MAIN POINTS / QUESTIONS TO ASK

- _____
- _____
- _____

CALL TO ACTION

_____

_____

_____

_____

_____

Episode Details

TITLE: _____

GUEST: _____

TOPIC: _____

RECORDING DATE: _____

PUBLISHED DATE: _____

EPISODE #: _____

EP LENGTH: _____

RECORDING LIST

- ☐ _____
- ☐ _____
- ☐ _____
- ☐ _____
- ☐ _____
- ☐ _____
- ☐ _____

EDITING LIST

- ☐ _____
- ☐ _____
- ☐ _____
- ☐ _____
- ☐ _____
- ☐ _____
- ☐ _____

PUBLISHING LIST

- ☐ _____
- ☐ _____
- ☐ _____
- ☐ _____
- ☐ _____
- ☐ _____
- ☐ _____

INTRO

_____
_____
_____

IDEAS / INTERVIEW QUESTIONS

_____
_____
_____
_____
_____
_____
_____
_____
_____
_____
_____
_____
_____
_____
_____

SHOW NOTES

_____
_____
_____
_____
_____
_____
_____
_____
_____
_____

OUTRO

_____
_____
_____

Episode Planner

BIO:

_____
Title

CONTACT:

_____

_____

_____

_____

_____

_____

_____

_____

_____

_____

_____

_____

Topic

_____

_____

_____

WEBSITE:

_____

_____

_____

SOCIAL MEDIA:

_____

_____

_____

Guest

MAIN POINTS / QUESTIONS TO ASK

- _____
- _____
- _____

CALL TO ACTION

_____

_____

_____

_____

_____

_____

Episode Details

TITLE: _____

GUEST: _____

TOPIC: _____
_____

RECORDING DATE: _____

PUBLISHED DATE: _____

EPISODE #: _____

EP LENGTH: _____

RECORDING LIST

☐ _____
☐ _____
☐ _____
☐ _____
☐ _____
☐ _____
☐ _____

INTRO

_____
_____

IDEAS / INTERVIEW QUESTIONS

_____
_____
_____
_____
_____
_____
_____
_____
_____
_____
_____
_____
_____
_____
_____

EDITING LIST

☐ _____
☐ _____
☐ _____
☐ _____
☐ _____
☐ _____
☐ _____

SHOW NOTES

_____
_____
_____
_____
_____
_____
_____
_____
_____
_____
_____

PUBLISHING LIST

☐ _____
☐ _____
☐ _____
☐ _____
☐ _____
☐ _____
☐ _____

OUTRO

_____
_____

Episode Planner

BIO:

_____

Title

CONTACT:

_____

WEBSITE:

_____

Topic

_____

SOCIAL MEDIA:

_____

Guest

MAIN POINTS / QUESTIONS TO ASK

- _____
- _____
- _____

CALL TO ACTION

_____

Episode Details

TITLE: _____

GUEST: _____

TOPIC: _____

_____

RECORDING DATE: _____

PUBLISHED DATE: _____

EPISODE #: _____

EP LENGTH: _____

RECORDING LIST

☐ _____
☐ _____
☐ _____
☐ _____
☐ _____
☐ _____
☐ _____

EDITING LIST

☐ _____
☐ _____
☐ _____
☐ _____
☐ _____
☐ _____
☐ _____

PUBLISHING LIST

☐ _____
☐ _____
☐ _____
☐ _____
☐ _____
☐ _____
☐ _____

INTRO

_____
_____
_____

IDEAS / INTERVIEW QUESTIONS

_____
_____
_____
_____
_____
_____
_____
_____
_____
_____
_____
_____
_____
_____

SHOW NOTES

_____
_____
_____
_____
_____
_____
_____
_____
_____
_____

OUTRO

_____
_____

Episode Planner

BIO:

_____

_____

_____

_____

_____

_____

_____

_____

_____

_____

_____

_____

_____

_____

_____

_____

_____

_____

_____

_____
_____
Title

Topic

_____

_____

_____

_____
Guest

CONTACT:

_____

_____

_____

WEBSITE:

_____

_____

_____

SOCIAL MEDIA:

_____

_____

_____

MAIN POINTS / QUESTIONS TO ASK

- _____
- _____
- _____

CALL TO ACTION

_____

_____

_____

_____

_____

Episode Details

TITLE: _____

GUEST: _____

TOPIC: _____

RECORDING DATE: _____

PUBLISHED DATE: _____

EPISODE #: _____

EP LENGTH: _____

RECORDING LIST

- ☐ _____
- ☐ _____
- ☐ _____
- ☐ _____
- ☐ _____
- ☐ _____
- ☐ _____

EDITING LIST

- ☐ _____
- ☐ _____
- ☐ _____
- ☐ _____
- ☐ _____
- ☐ _____
- ☐ _____

PUBLISHING LIST

- ☐ _____
- ☐ _____
- ☐ _____
- ☐ _____
- ☐ _____
- ☐ _____

INTRO

_____
_____
_____

IDEAS / INTERVIEW QUESTIONS

_____
_____
_____
_____
_____
_____
_____
_____
_____
_____
_____
_____
_____
_____

SHOW NOTES

_____
_____
_____
_____
_____
_____
_____
_____
_____
_____
_____
_____

OUTRO

_____
_____
_____

Episode Planner

BIO:

Title

CONTACT:

Topic

WEBSITE:

SOCIAL MEDIA:

Guest

MAIN POINTS / QUESTIONS TO ASK

- _____
- _____
- _____

CALL TO ACTION

Episode Details

TITLE: _____

GUEST: _____

TOPIC: _____
_____

RECORDING DATE: _____

PUBLISHED DATE: _____

EPISODE #: _____

EP LENGTH: _____

RECORDING LIST

- ☐ _____
- ☐ _____
- ☐ _____
- ☐ _____
- ☐ _____
- ☐ _____
- ☐ _____

EDITING LIST

- ☐ _____
- ☐ _____
- ☐ _____
- ☐ _____
- ☐ _____
- ☐ _____
- ☐ _____

PUBLISHING LIST

- ☐ _____
- ☐ _____
- ☐ _____
- ☐ _____
- ☐ _____
- ☐ _____
- ☐ _____

INTRO

_____
_____
_____

IDEAS / INTERVIEW QUESTIONS

_____
_____
_____
_____
_____
_____
_____
_____
_____
_____
_____
_____
_____
_____
_____

SHOW NOTES

_____
_____
_____
_____
_____
_____
_____
_____
_____
_____
_____
_____

OUTRO

_____
_____
_____

Episode Planner

BIO:

_____

_____

_____

_____

_____

_____

_____

_____

_____

_____

_____

_____

_____

_____

_____

_____

_____

_____

_____

Title

Topic

_____

_____

_____

_____

Guest

CONTACT:

_____

_____

_____

WEBSITE:

_____

_____

_____

SOCIAL MEDIA:

_____

_____

_____

MAIN POINTS / QUESTIONS TO ASK

- _____

- _____

- _____

CALL TO ACTION

_____

_____

_____

_____

_____

Episode Details

TITLE: _____

GUEST: _____

TOPIC: _____
_____

RECORDING DATE: _____

PUBLISHED DATE: _____

EPISODE #: _____

EP LENGTH: _____

RECORDING LIST

- ☐ _____
- ☐ _____
- ☐ _____
- ☐ _____
- ☐ _____
- ☐ _____
- ☐ _____

EDITING LIST

- ☐ _____
- ☐ _____
- ☐ _____
- ☐ _____
- ☐ _____
- ☐ _____
- ☐ _____

PUBLISHING LIST

- ☐ _____
- ☐ _____
- ☐ _____
- ☐ _____
- ☐ _____
- ☐ _____
- ☐ _____

INTRO

_____
_____
_____

IDEAS / INTERVIEW QUESTIONS

_____
_____
_____
_____
_____
_____
_____
_____
_____
_____
_____
_____

SHOW NOTES

_____
_____
_____
_____
_____
_____
_____
_____
_____
_____
_____
_____

OUTRO

_____
_____
_____

Episode Planner

PURPOSE: INSPIRE / EDUCATE / ENTERTAIN

BIO:

_____
Title

Topic

CONTACT:

WEBSITE:

SOCIAL MEDIA:

_____
Guest

MAIN POINTS / QUESTIONS TO ASK

- _____
- _____
- _____

CALL TO ACTION

Episode Details

TITLE: _____

GUEST: _____

TOPIC: _____

RECORDING DATE: _____

PUBLISHED DATE: _____

EPISODE #: _____

EP LENGTH: _____

RECORDING LIST

- ☐ _____
- ☐ _____
- ☐ _____
- ☐ _____
- ☐ _____
- ☐ _____
- ☐ _____

EDITING LIST

- ☐ _____
- ☐ _____
- ☐ _____
- ☐ _____
- ☐ _____
- ☐ _____
- ☐ _____

PUBLISHING LIST

- ☐ _____
- ☐ _____
- ☐ _____
- ☐ _____
- ☐ _____
- ☐ _____
- ☐ _____

INTRO

_____
_____
_____

IDEAS / INTERVIEW QUESTIONS

_____
_____
_____
_____
_____
_____
_____
_____
_____
_____
_____
_____
_____
_____
_____
_____

SHOW NOTES

_____
_____
_____
_____
_____
_____
_____
_____
_____
_____
_____
_____

OUTRO

_____
_____
_____

Episode Planner

BIO:

_____

_____

Title

_____

_____

Topic

_____

_____

_____

CONTACT:

_____

_____

WEBSITE:

_____

_____

SOCIAL MEDIA:

_____

_____

Guest

MAIN POINTS / QUESTIONS TO ASK

- _____
- _____
- _____

CALL TO ACTION

_____

_____

_____

_____

Episode Details

TITLE: _____

GUEST: _____

TOPIC: _____

RECORDING DATE: _____

PUBLISHED DATE: _____

EPISODE #: _____

EP LENGTH: _____

RECORDING LIST

- ☐ _____
- ☐ _____
- ☐ _____
- ☐ _____
- ☐ _____
- ☐ _____
- ☐ _____

EDITING LIST

- ☐ _____
- ☐ _____
- ☐ _____
- ☐ _____
- ☐ _____
- ☐ _____
- ☐ _____

PUBLISHING LIST

- ☐ _____
- ☐ _____
- ☐ _____
- ☐ _____
- ☐ _____
- ☐ _____
- ☐ _____

INTRO

_____

_____

_____

IDEAS / INTERVIEW QUESTIONS

_____

_____

_____

_____

_____

_____

_____

_____

_____

_____

_____

_____

_____

_____

_____

SHOW NOTES

_____

_____

_____

_____

_____

_____

_____

_____

_____

_____

_____

OUTRO

_____

_____

_____

_____

Episode Planner

BIO:

_____
_____
_____
_____
_____
_____
_____
_____
_____
_____
_____

_____
Title

Topic

_____
_____
_____

CONTACT:

_____
_____
_____

WEBSITE:

_____
_____

SOCIAL MEDIA:

_____
_____
_____

_____
Guest

MAIN POINTS / QUESTIONS TO ASK

- _____
- _____
- _____

CALL TO ACTION

_____
_____
_____
_____
_____
_____

Episode Details

TITLE: _____   RECORDING DATE: _____

GUEST: _____   PUBLISHED DATE: _____

TOPIC: _____   EPISODE #: _____

_____   EP LENGTH: _____

RECORDING LIST

- ☐ _____
- ☐ _____
- ☐ _____
- ☐ _____
- ☐ _____
- ☐ _____
- ☐ _____

EDITING LIST

- ☐ _____
- ☐ _____
- ☐ _____
- ☐ _____
- ☐ _____
- ☐ _____
- ☐ _____

PUBLISHING LIST

- ☐ _____
- ☐ _____
- ☐ _____
- ☐ _____
- ☐ _____
- ☐ _____

INTRO

_____
_____
_____

IDEAS / INTERVIEW QUESTIONS

_____
_____
_____
_____
_____
_____
_____
_____
_____
_____
_____
_____
_____
_____
_____
_____
_____

SHOW NOTES

_____
_____
_____
_____
_____
_____
_____
_____
_____
_____
_____
_____

OUTRO

_____
_____

Episode Planner

BIO:

_____

Title

CONTACT:

Topic

_____

_____

_____

WEBSITE:

SOCIAL MEDIA:

_____

Guest

MAIN POINTS / QUESTIONS TO ASK

- _____
- _____
- _____

CALL TO ACTION

Episode Details

TITLE: _____   RECORDING DATE: _____

GUEST: _____   PUBLISHED DATE: _____

TOPIC: _____   EPISODE #: _____

_____   EP LENGTH: _____

RECORDING LIST

- ☐ _____
- ☐ _____
- ☐ _____
- ☐ _____
- ☐ _____
- ☐ _____
- ☐ _____

EDITING LIST

- ☐ _____
- ☐ _____
- ☐ _____
- ☐ _____
- ☐ _____
- ☐ _____
- ☐ _____

PUBLISHING LIST

- ☐ _____
- ☐ _____
- ☐ _____
- ☐ _____
- ☐ _____
- ☐ _____
- ☐ _____

INTRO

_____
_____
_____

IDEAS / INTERVIEW QUESTIONS

_____
_____
_____
_____
_____
_____
_____
_____
_____
_____
_____
_____
_____
_____
_____
_____

SHOW NOTES

_____
_____
_____
_____
_____
_____
_____
_____
_____
_____
_____
_____

OUTRO

_____
_____
_____

Episode Planner

BIO:

_____
Title

CONTACT:

Topic

_____
_____
_____

WEBSITE:

SOCIAL MEDIA:

Guest

MAIN POINTS / QUESTIONS TO ASK

- _____
- _____
- _____

CALL TO ACTION

Episode Details

TITLE: _____

GUEST: _____

TOPIC: _____
_____

RECORDING DATE: _____

PUBLISHED DATE: _____

EPISODE #: _____

EP LENGTH: _____

RECORDING LIST

- ☐ _____
- ☐ _____
- ☐ _____
- ☐ _____
- ☐ _____
- ☐ _____
- ☐ _____

EDITING LIST

- ☐ _____
- ☐ _____
- ☐ _____
- ☐ _____
- ☐ _____
- ☐ _____
- ☐ _____

PUBLISHING LIST

- ☐ _____
- ☐ _____
- ☐ _____
- ☐ _____
- ☐ _____
- ☐ _____
- ☐ _____

INTRO

_____
_____
_____

IDEAS / INTERVIEW QUESTIONS

_____
_____
_____
_____
_____
_____
_____
_____
_____
_____
_____
_____
_____

SHOW NOTES

_____
_____
_____
_____
_____
_____
_____
_____
_____
_____
_____

OUTRO

_____
_____
_____

Episode Planner

BIO:

CONTACT:

_____
Title

Topic

_____
_____
_____

WEBSITE:

SOCIAL MEDIA:

Guest

MAIN POINTS / QUESTIONS TO ASK

- _____
- _____
- _____

CALL TO ACTION

_____
_____
_____
_____
_____

Episode Details

TITLE: _____ RECORDING DATE: _____

GUEST: _____ PUBLISHED DATE: _____

TOPIC: _____ EPISODE #: _____

EP LENGTH: _____

RECORDING LIST

☐ _____
☐ _____
☐ _____
☐ _____
☐ _____
☐ _____
☐ _____

EDITING LIST

☐ _____
☐ _____
☐ _____
☐ _____
☐ _____
☐ _____
☐ _____

PUBLISHING LIST

☐ _____
☐ _____
☐ _____
☐ _____
☐ _____
☐ _____
☐ _____

INTRO

_____
_____
_____

IDEAS / INTERVIEW QUESTIONS

_____
_____
_____
_____
_____
_____
_____
_____
_____
_____
_____
_____
_____
_____
_____

SHOW NOTES

_____
_____
_____
_____
_____
_____
_____
_____
_____
_____
_____

OUTRO

_____
_____
_____

Episode Planner

BIO:
_____
_____
_____
_____
_____
_____
_____
_____
_____
_____
_____
_____

_____
Title

Topic

_____
_____
_____

_____
Guest

CONTACT:
_____
_____

WEBSITE:
_____
_____
_____

SOCIAL MEDIA:
_____
_____
_____

MAIN POINTS / QUESTIONS TO ASK

- _____
- _____
- _____

CALL TO ACTION

_____
_____
_____
_____
_____

Episode Details

TITLE: _____

GUEST: _____

TOPIC: _____

_____

RECORDING DATE: _____

PUBLISHED DATE: _____

EPISODE #: _____

EP LENGTH: _____

RECORDING LIST

- ☐ _____
- ☐ _____
- ☐ _____
- ☐ _____
- ☐ _____
- ☐ _____
- ☐ _____

EDITING LIST

- ☐ _____
- ☐ _____
- ☐ _____
- ☐ _____
- ☐ _____
- ☐ _____
- ☐ _____

PUBLISHING LIST

- ☐ _____
- ☐ _____
- ☐ _____
- ☐ _____
- ☐ _____
- ☐ _____
- ☐ _____

INTRO

_____

_____

IDEAS / INTERVIEW QUESTIONS

_____

_____

_____

_____

_____

_____

_____

_____

_____

_____

_____

_____

_____

SHOW NOTES

_____

_____

_____

_____

_____

_____

_____

_____

_____

_____

_____

_____

OUTRO

_____

_____

_____

Episode Planner

PURPOSE: INSPIRE / EDUCATE / ENTERTAIN

BIO:

_____

_____

_____

_____

_____

_____

_____

_____

_____

_____

_____

CONTACT:

_____

_____

WEBSITE:

_____

_____

SOCIAL MEDIA:

_____

_____

_____

Title

Topic

_____

_____

_____

Guest

MAIN POINTS / QUESTIONS TO ASK

- _____
- _____
- _____

CALL TO ACTION

_____

_____

_____

_____

Episode Details

TITLE: _____

GUEST: _____

TOPIC: _____

RECORDING DATE: _____

PUBLISHED DATE: _____

EPISODE #: _____

EP LENGTH: _____

RECORDING LIST

- ☐ _____
- ☐ _____
- ☐ _____
- ☐ _____
- ☐ _____
- ☐ _____
- ☐ _____

EDITING LIST

- ☐ _____
- ☐ _____
- ☐ _____
- ☐ _____
- ☐ _____
- ☐ _____
- ☐ _____

PUBLISHING LIST

- ☐ _____
- ☐ _____
- ☐ _____
- ☐ _____
- ☐ _____
- ☐ _____
- ☐ _____

INTRO

_____

_____

IDEAS / INTERVIEW QUESTIONS

_____

_____

_____

_____

_____

_____

_____

_____

_____

_____

_____

_____

SHOW NOTES

_____

_____

_____

_____

_____

_____

_____

_____

_____

_____

OUTRO

_____

_____

_____

Episode Planner

PURPOSE: INSPIRE / EDUCATE / ENTERTAIN

BIO:

_____
Title

CONTACT:

Topic

_____
_____
_____

WEBSITE:

SOCIAL MEDIA:

Guest

MAIN POINTS / QUESTIONS TO ASK

- _____
- _____
- _____

CALL TO ACTION

Episode Details

TITLE: _____
GUEST: _____

RECORDING DATE: _____
PUBLISHED DATE: _____

TOPIC: _____

EPISODE #: _____
EP LENGTH: _____

RECORDING LIST

☐ _____
☐ _____
☐ _____
☐ _____
☐ _____
☐ _____
☐ _____

EDITING LIST

☐ _____
☐ _____
☐ _____
☐ _____
☐ _____
☐ _____
☐ _____

PUBLISHING LIST

☐ _____
☐ _____
☐ _____
☐ _____
☐ _____
☐ _____
☐ _____

INTRO

_____
_____
_____

IDEAS / INTERVIEW QUESTIONS

_____
_____
_____
_____
_____
_____
_____
_____
_____
_____
_____
_____
_____
_____
_____
_____

SHOW NOTES

_____
_____
_____
_____
_____
_____
_____
_____
_____
_____
_____

OUTRO

_____
_____
_____

Episode Planner

BIO:

Title

CONTACT:

Topic

WEBSITE:

SOCIAL MEDIA:

Guest

MAIN POINTS / QUESTIONS TO ASK

• _____
• _____
• _____

CALL TO ACTION

Episode Details

TITLE: _____

GUEST: _____

TOPIC: _____
_____

RECORDING DATE: _____

PUBLISHED DATE: _____

EPISODE #: _____

EP LENGTH: _____

RECORDING LIST

☐ _____
☐ _____
☐ _____
☐ _____
☐ _____
☐ _____
☐ _____

EDITING LIST

☐ _____
☐ _____
☐ _____
☐ _____
☐ _____
☐ _____
☐ _____

PUBLISHING LIST

☐ _____
☐ _____
☐ _____
☐ _____
☐ _____
☐ _____
☐ _____

INTRO

_____
_____
_____

IDEAS / INTERVIEW QUESTIONS

_____
_____
_____
_____
_____
_____
_____
_____
_____
_____
_____
_____
_____
_____
_____

SHOW NOTES

_____
_____
_____
_____
_____
_____
_____
_____
_____
_____
_____

OUTRO

_____
_____
_____

Episode Planner

BIO:

_____

Title

CONTACT:

Topic

WEBSITE:

SOCIAL MEDIA:

Guest

MAIN POINTS / QUESTIONS TO ASK

• _____

• _____

• _____

CALL TO ACTION

_____
_____
_____
_____
_____

Episode Details

TITLE: _____

GUEST: _____

TOPIC: _____
_____

RECORDING DATE: _____

PUBLISHED DATE: _____

EPISODE #: _____

EP LENGTH: _____

RECORDING LIST

☐ _____
☐ _____
☐ _____
☐ _____
☐ _____
☐ _____
☐ _____

EDITING LIST

☐ _____
☐ _____
☐ _____
☐ _____
☐ _____
☐ _____
☐ _____

PUBLISHING LIST

☐ _____
☐ _____
☐ _____
☐ _____
☐ _____
☐ _____
☐ _____

INTRO

_____
_____
_____

IDEAS / INTERVIEW QUESTIONS

_____
_____
_____
_____
_____
_____
_____
_____
_____
_____
_____
_____
_____
_____
_____

SHOW NOTES

_____
_____
_____
_____
_____
_____
_____
_____
_____
_____
_____
_____
_____

OUTRO

_____
_____
_____

Episode Planner

BIO:

_____

CONTACT:

_____ *Title*

_____
_____
_____
_____
_____
_____

Topic

_____
_____
_____

WEBSITE:

_____
_____
_____

SOCIAL MEDIA:

_____
_____
_____

_____
_____

Guest

MAIN POINTS / QUESTIONS TO ASK

• _____

• _____

• _____

CALL TO ACTION

_____
_____
_____
_____
_____

Episode Details

TITLE: _____   RECORDING DATE: _____

GUEST: _____   PUBLISHED DATE: _____

TOPIC: _____   EPISODE #: _____

_____   EP LENGTH: _____

RECORDING LIST

- ☐ _____
- ☐ _____
- ☐ _____
- ☐ _____
- ☐ _____
- ☐ _____
- ☐ _____

EDITING LIST

- ☐ _____
- ☐ _____
- ☐ _____
- ☐ _____
- ☐ _____
- ☐ _____
- ☐ _____

PUBLISHING LIST

- ☐ _____
- ☐ _____
- ☐ _____
- ☐ _____
- ☐ _____
- ☐ _____
- ☐ _____

INTRO

_____
_____
_____

IDEAS / INTERVIEW QUESTIONS

_____
_____
_____
_____
_____
_____
_____
_____
_____
_____
_____
_____
_____
_____

SHOW NOTES

_____
_____
_____
_____
_____
_____
_____
_____
_____
_____
_____
_____

OUTRO

_____
_____
_____

Episode Planner

PURPOSE: INSPIRE / EDUCATE / ENTERTAIN

BIO:

_____

Title

CONTACT:

Topic

WEBSITE:

SOCIAL MEDIA:

Guest

MAIN POINTS / QUESTIONS TO ASK

- _____
- _____
- _____

CALL TO ACTION

Episode Details

TITLE: _____

GUEST: _____

TOPIC: _____

RECORDING DATE: _____

PUBLISHED DATE: _____

EPISODE #: _____

EP LENGTH: _____

RECORDING LIST

- [ ] _____
- [ ] _____
- [ ] _____
- [ ] _____
- [ ] _____
- [ ] _____
- [ ] _____

EDITING LIST

- [ ] _____
- [ ] _____
- [ ] _____
- [ ] _____
- [ ] _____
- [ ] _____
- [ ] _____

PUBLISHING LIST

- [ ] _____
- [ ] _____
- [ ] _____
- [ ] _____
- [ ] _____
- [ ] _____
- [ ] _____

INTRO

_____
_____
_____

IDEAS / INTERVIEW QUESTIONS

_____
_____
_____
_____
_____
_____
_____
_____
_____
_____
_____
_____
_____
_____
_____
_____
_____
_____

SHOW NOTES

_____
_____
_____
_____
_____
_____
_____
_____
_____
_____
_____
_____

OUTRO

_____
_____
_____

Episode Planner

PURPOSE: INSPIRE / EDUCATE / ENTERTAIN

BIO: _____

_____

Title

CONTACT:

_____

_____

Topic

WEBSITE:

_____

_____

SOCIAL MEDIA:

_____

Guest

MAIN POINTS / QUESTIONS TO ASK

- _____
- _____
- _____

CALL TO ACTION

_____

Episode Details

TITLE: _____
GUEST: _____
TOPIC: _____

RECORDING DATE: _____
PUBLISHED DATE: _____
EPISODE #: _____
EP LENGTH: _____

RECORDING LIST

- [ ] _____
- [ ] _____
- [ ] _____
- [ ] _____
- [ ] _____
- [ ] _____
- [ ] _____

EDITING LIST

- [ ] _____
- [ ] _____
- [ ] _____
- [ ] _____
- [ ] _____
- [ ] _____
- [ ] _____

PUBLISHING LIST

- [ ] _____
- [ ] _____
- [ ] _____
- [ ] _____
- [ ] _____
- [ ] _____
- [ ] _____

INTRO

_____
_____
_____

IDEAS / INTERVIEW QUESTIONS

_____
_____
_____
_____
_____
_____
_____
_____
_____
_____
_____
_____
_____
_____
_____
_____
_____

SHOW NOTES

_____
_____
_____
_____
_____
_____
_____
_____
_____
_____
_____
_____

OUTRO

_____
_____
_____

Episode Planner

BIO:

_____
Title

CONTACT:

Topic

_____

_____

_____

WEBSITE:

SOCIAL MEDIA:

_____
Guest

MAIN POINTS / QUESTIONS TO ASK

- _____
- _____
- _____

CALL TO ACTION

Episode Details

TITLE: _____

GUEST: _____

TOPIC: _____

RECORDING DATE: _____

PUBLISHED DATE: _____

EPISODE #: _____

EP LENGTH: _____

RECORDING LIST

- ☐ _____
- ☐ _____
- ☐ _____
- ☐ _____
- ☐ _____
- ☐ _____
- ☐ _____

EDITING LIST

- ☐ _____
- ☐ _____
- ☐ _____
- ☐ _____
- ☐ _____
- ☐ _____
- ☐ _____

PUBLISHING LIST

- ☐ _____
- ☐ _____
- ☐ _____
- ☐ _____
- ☐ _____
- ☐ _____
- ☐ _____

INTRO

_____
_____
_____

IDEAS / INTERVIEW QUESTIONS

_____
_____
_____
_____
_____
_____
_____
_____
_____
_____
_____
_____
_____
_____
_____
_____
_____

SHOW NOTES

_____
_____
_____
_____
_____
_____
_____
_____
_____
_____
_____
_____

OUTRO

_____
_____
_____

Episode Planner

PURPOSE: INSPIRE / EDUCATE / ENTERTAIN

BIO:

_____
Title

CONTACT:

Topic

WEBSITE:

SOCIAL MEDIA:

Guest

MAIN POINTS / QUESTIONS TO ASK

- _____
- _____
- _____

CALL TO ACTION

Episode Details

TITLE: _____

GUEST: _____

TOPIC: _____
_____

RECORDING DATE: _____

PUBLISHED DATE: _____

EPISODE #: _____

EP LENGTH: _____

RECORDING LIST

- ☐ _____
- ☐ _____
- ☐ _____
- ☐ _____
- ☐ _____
- ☐ _____
- ☐ _____

EDITING LIST

- ☐ _____
- ☐ _____
- ☐ _____
- ☐ _____
- ☐ _____
- ☐ _____
- ☐ _____

PUBLISHING LIST

- ☐ _____
- ☐ _____
- ☐ _____
- ☐ _____
- ☐ _____
- ☐ _____
- ☐ _____

INTRO

_____
_____
_____

IDEAS / INTERVIEW QUESTIONS

_____
_____
_____
_____
_____
_____
_____
_____
_____
_____
_____
_____
_____
_____
_____
_____

SHOW NOTES

_____
_____
_____
_____
_____
_____
_____
_____
_____
_____
_____
_____
_____

OUTRO

_____
_____
_____

Episode Planner

BIO: _____ _Title_ _____ CONTACT:
_____   _____
_____   _____
_____
_____   _____
_____
_____   _Topic_
_____
_____   _____   WEBSITE:
_____   _____   _____
_____   _____   _____
_____   _____
_____
_____   SOCIAL MEDIA:
_____   _____
_____   _____
_____   _____

_____
Guest

MAIN POINTS / QUESTIONS TO ASK

- _____
- _____
- _____

CALL TO ACTION

_____
_____
_____
_____
_____

Episode Details

TITLE: _____

GUEST: _____

TOPIC: _____
_____

RECORDING DATE: _____

PUBLISHED DATE: _____

EPISODE #: _____

EP LENGTH: _____

RECORDING LIST

- ☐ _____
- ☐ _____
- ☐ _____
- ☐ _____
- ☐ _____
- ☐ _____
- ☐ _____

EDITING LIST

- ☐ _____
- ☐ _____
- ☐ _____
- ☐ _____
- ☐ _____
- ☐ _____
- ☐ _____

PUBLISHING LIST

- ☐ _____
- ☐ _____
- ☐ _____
- ☐ _____
- ☐ _____
- ☐ _____
- ☐ _____

INTRO

_____
_____
_____

IDEAS / INTERVIEW QUESTIONS

_____
_____
_____
_____
_____
_____
_____
_____
_____
_____
_____
_____
_____
_____
_____
_____
_____

SHOW NOTES

_____
_____
_____
_____
_____
_____
_____
_____
_____
_____
_____

OUTRO

_____
_____
_____

Episode Planner

BIO:
_____
_____
_____
_____
_____
_____
_____
_____
_____
_____
_____

_____
Title

Topic
_____
_____
_____

Guest

CONTACT:
_____
_____

WEBSITE:
_____
_____

SOCIAL MEDIA:
_____
_____
_____

MAIN POINTS / QUESTIONS TO ASK

- _____
- _____
- _____

CALL TO ACTION

_____
_____
_____
_____
_____
_____

Episode Details

TITLE: _____

GUEST: _____

TOPIC: _____

RECORDING DATE: _____

PUBLISHED DATE: _____

EPISODE #: _____

EP LENGTH: _____

RECORDING LIST

☐ _____
☐ _____
☐ _____
☐ _____
☐ _____
☐ _____
☐ _____

EDITING LIST

☐ _____
☐ _____
☐ _____
☐ _____
☐ _____
☐ _____
☐ _____

PUBLISHING LIST

☐ _____
☐ _____
☐ _____
☐ _____
☐ _____
☐ _____
☐ _____

INTRO

_____
_____
_____

IDEAS / INTERVIEW QUESTIONS

_____
_____
_____
_____
_____
_____
_____
_____
_____
_____
_____
_____
_____
_____

SHOW NOTES

_____
_____
_____
_____
_____
_____
_____
_____
_____
_____

OUTRO

_____
_____
_____

Episode Planner

BIO:
_____
Title
_____
_____
_____
_____
_____
_____
_____
_____
_____
_____
_____
_____
_____

CONTACT:
_____
_____
_____

WEBSITE:
_____
_____

Topic
_____
_____
_____

SOCIAL MEDIA:
_____
_____
_____

Guest

MAIN POINTS / QUESTIONS TO ASK

- _____
- _____
- _____

CALL TO ACTION

_____
_____
_____
_____
_____

Episode Details

TITLE: _____ RECORDING DATE: _____

GUEST: _____ PUBLISHED DATE: _____

TOPIC: _____ EPISODE #: _____

   EP LENGTH: _____

RECORDING LIST

- ☐ _____
- ☐ _____
- ☐ _____
- ☐ _____
- ☐ _____
- ☐ _____
- ☐ _____

EDITING LIST

- ☐ _____
- ☐ _____
- ☐ _____
- ☐ _____
- ☐ _____
- ☐ _____
- ☐ _____

PUBLISHING LIST

- ☐ _____
- ☐ _____
- ☐ _____
- ☐ _____
- ☐ _____
- ☐ _____
- ☐ _____

INTRO

_____
_____
_____

IDEAS / INTERVIEW QUESTIONS

_____
_____
_____
_____
_____
_____
_____
_____
_____
_____
_____
_____
_____
_____
_____

SHOW NOTES

_____
_____
_____
_____
_____
_____
_____
_____
_____
_____
_____

OUTRO

_____
_____
_____

Episode Planner

BIO:

_____

Title

CONTACT:

Topic

WEBSITE:

SOCIAL MEDIA:

Guest

MAIN POINTS / QUESTIONS TO ASK

• _____

• _____

• _____

CALL TO ACTION

Episode Details

TITLE: _____ RECORDING DATE: _____

GUEST: _____ PUBLISHED DATE: _____

TOPIC: _____ EPISODE #: _____

EP LENGTH: _____

RECORDING LIST

- ☐ _____
- ☐ _____
- ☐ _____
- ☐ _____
- ☐ _____
- ☐ _____
- ☐ _____

EDITING LIST

- ☐ _____
- ☐ _____
- ☐ _____
- ☐ _____
- ☐ _____
- ☐ _____
- ☐ _____

PUBLISHING LIST

- ☐ _____
- ☐ _____
- ☐ _____
- ☐ _____
- ☐ _____
- ☐ _____
- ☐ _____

INTRO

_____
_____
_____

IDEAS / INTERVIEW QUESTIONS

_____
_____
_____
_____
_____
_____
_____
_____
_____
_____
_____
_____
_____

SHOW NOTES

_____
_____
_____
_____
_____
_____
_____
_____
_____
_____
_____

OUTRO

_____
_____
_____

Episode Planner

BIO: _____
_____
_____ *Title*
_____
_____
_____
_____ *Topic*
_____ _____
_____ _____
_____ _____
_____
_____
_____
_____
_____

CONTACT:
_____
_____

WEBSITE:
_____
_____

SOCIAL MEDIA:
_____
_____
_____

Guest

MAIN POINTS / QUESTIONS TO ASK

- _____
- _____
- _____

CALL TO ACTION

_____
_____
_____
_____
_____

Episode Details

TITLE: _____

GUEST: _____

TOPIC: _____

RECORDING DATE: _____

PUBLISHED DATE: _____

EPISODE #: _____

EP LENGTH: _____

RECORDING LIST

☐ _____
☐ _____
☐ _____
☐ _____
☐ _____
☐ _____
☐ _____

EDITING LIST

☐ _____
☐ _____
☐ _____
☐ _____
☐ _____
☐ _____
☐ _____

PUBLISHING LIST

☐ _____
☐ _____
☐ _____
☐ _____
☐ _____
☐ _____

INTRO

_____
_____
_____

IDEAS / INTERVIEW QUESTIONS

_____
_____
_____
_____
_____
_____
_____
_____
_____
_____
_____
_____
_____
_____
_____
_____

SHOW NOTES

_____
_____
_____
_____
_____
_____
_____
_____
_____

OUTRO

_____
_____
_____

Episode Planner

BIO:
_____
_____
_____
_____
_____
_____
_____
_____
_____
_____
_____

_____
Title

Topic
_____
_____
_____

_____
Guest

CONTACT:
_____
_____

WEBSITE:
_____
_____

SOCIAL MEDIA:
_____
_____
_____

MAIN POINTS / QUESTIONS TO ASK

- _____
- _____
- _____

CALL TO ACTION

_____
_____
_____
_____
_____

Episode Details

TITLE: _____ RECORDING DATE: _____

GUEST: _____ PUBLISHED DATE: _____

TOPIC: _____ EPISODE #: _____

EP LENGTH: _____

RECORDING LIST

- ☐ _____
- ☐ _____
- ☐ _____
- ☐ _____
- ☐ _____
- ☐ _____
- ☐ _____

INTRO

_____
_____
_____

IDEAS / INTERVIEW QUESTIONS

_____
_____
_____
_____
_____
_____
_____
_____
_____
_____
_____
_____
_____
_____

EDITING LIST

- ☐ _____
- ☐ _____
- ☐ _____
- ☐ _____
- ☐ _____
- ☐ _____
- ☐ _____

SHOW NOTES

_____
_____
_____
_____
_____
_____
_____
_____
_____
_____

PUBLISHING LIST

- ☐ _____
- ☐ _____
- ☐ _____
- ☐ _____
- ☐ _____
- ☐ _____
- ☐ _____

OUTRO

_____
_____
_____

Episode Planner

BIO:

_____
Title

CONTACT:

Topic

_____
_____
_____

WEBSITE:

SOCIAL MEDIA:

Guest

MAIN POINTS / QUESTIONS TO ASK

- _____
- _____
- _____

CALL TO ACTION

_____
_____
_____
_____
_____

Episode Details

TITLE: _____

GUEST: _____

TOPIC: _____
_____

RECORDING DATE: _____

PUBLISHED DATE: _____

EPISODE #: _____

EP LENGTH: _____

RECORDING LIST

- ☐ _____
- ☐ _____
- ☐ _____
- ☐ _____
- ☐ _____
- ☐ _____
- ☐ _____

EDITING LIST

- ☐ _____
- ☐ _____
- ☐ _____
- ☐ _____
- ☐ _____
- ☐ _____
- ☐ _____

PUBLISHING LIST

- ☐ _____
- ☐ _____
- ☐ _____
- ☐ _____
- ☐ _____
- ☐ _____
- ☐ _____

INTRO

_____
_____
_____

IDEAS / INTERVIEW QUESTIONS

_____
_____
_____
_____
_____
_____
_____
_____
_____
_____
_____
_____
_____
_____

SHOW NOTES

_____
_____
_____
_____
_____
_____
_____
_____
_____
_____
_____
_____

OUTRO

_____
_____
_____

Episode Planner

BIO:
_____
_____
_____
_____
_____
_____
_____
_____
_____
_____

_____
Title

Topic
_____
_____
_____

_____
Guest

CONTACT:
_____
_____
_____

WEBSITE:
_____
_____
_____

SOCIAL MEDIA:
_____
_____
_____

MAIN POINTS / QUESTIONS TO ASK

- _____
- _____
- _____

CALL TO ACTION

_____
_____
_____
_____
_____

Episode Details

TITLE: _____

GUEST: _____

TOPIC: _____

RECORDING DATE: _____

PUBLISHED DATE: _____

EPISODE #: _____

EP LENGTH: _____

RECORDING LIST

- ☐ _____
- ☐ _____
- ☐ _____
- ☐ _____
- ☐ _____
- ☐ _____
- ☐ _____

EDITING LIST

- ☐ _____
- ☐ _____
- ☐ _____
- ☐ _____
- ☐ _____
- ☐ _____
- ☐ _____

PUBLISHING LIST

- ☐ _____
- ☐ _____
- ☐ _____
- ☐ _____
- ☐ _____
- ☐ _____
- ☐ _____

INTRO

_____
_____
_____

IDEAS / INTERVIEW QUESTIONS

_____
_____
_____
_____
_____
_____
_____
_____
_____
_____
_____
_____
_____
_____

SHOW NOTES

_____
_____
_____
_____
_____
_____
_____
_____
_____
_____

OUTRO

_____
_____
_____

Episode Planner

BIO:
_____
_____
_____
_____
_____
_____
_____
_____
_____
_____
_____
_____

_____
Title

Topic
_____
_____
_____

_____
Guest

CONTACT:
_____
_____

WEBSITE:
_____
_____

SOCIAL MEDIA:
_____
_____
_____

MAIN POINTS / QUESTIONS TO ASK

- _____
- _____
- _____

CALL TO ACTION

_____
_____
_____
_____
_____
_____

Episode Details

TITLE: _____

GUEST: _____

TOPIC: _____

RECORDING DATE: _____

PUBLISHED DATE: _____

EPISODE #: _____

EP LENGTH: _____

RECORDING LIST

- ☐ _____
- ☐ _____
- ☐ _____
- ☐ _____
- ☐ _____
- ☐ _____
- ☐ _____

EDITING LIST

- ☐ _____
- ☐ _____
- ☐ _____
- ☐ _____
- ☐ _____
- ☐ _____
- ☐ _____

PUBLISHING LIST

- ☐ _____
- ☐ _____
- ☐ _____
- ☐ _____
- ☐ _____
- ☐ _____
- ☐ _____

INTRO

_____
_____
_____

IDEAS / INTERVIEW QUESTIONS

_____
_____
_____
_____
_____
_____
_____
_____
_____
_____
_____
_____
_____
_____
_____

SHOW NOTES

_____
_____
_____
_____
_____
_____
_____
_____
_____
_____
_____

OUTRO

_____
_____
_____

Episode Planner

BIO:

_____
Title

CONTACT:

Topic

WEBSITE:

SOCIAL MEDIA:

_____
Guest

MAIN POINTS / QUESTIONS TO ASK

• _____

• _____

• _____

CALL TO ACTION

Episode Details

TITLE: _____   RECORDING DATE: _____

GUEST: _____   PUBLISHED DATE: _____

TOPIC: _____   EPISODE #: _____

EP LENGTH: _____

RECORDING LIST

- ☐ _____
- ☐ _____
- ☐ _____
- ☐ _____
- ☐ _____
- ☐ _____
- ☐ _____

EDITING LIST

- ☐ _____
- ☐ _____
- ☐ _____
- ☐ _____
- ☐ _____
- ☐ _____
- ☐ _____

PUBLISHING LIST

- ☐ _____
- ☐ _____
- ☐ _____
- ☐ _____
- ☐ _____
- ☐ _____
- ☐ _____

INTRO

_____
_____
_____

IDEAS / INTERVIEW QUESTIONS

_____
_____
_____
_____
_____
_____
_____
_____
_____
_____
_____
_____

SHOW NOTES

_____
_____
_____
_____
_____
_____
_____
_____
_____
_____
_____

OUTRO

_____
_____
_____

Episode Planner

PURPOSE: INSPIRE / EDUCATE / ENTERTAIN

BIO:

_____
Title

CONTACT:

Topic

WEBSITE:

SOCIAL MEDIA:

Guest

MAIN POINTS / QUESTIONS TO ASK

- _____
- _____
- _____

CALL TO ACTION

Episode Details

TITLE: _____

GUEST: _____

TOPIC: _____

RECORDING DATE: _____

PUBLISHED DATE: _____

EPISODE #: _____

EP LENGTH: _____

RECORDING LIST

- ☐ _____
- ☐ _____
- ☐ _____
- ☐ _____
- ☐ _____
- ☐ _____
- ☐ _____

EDITING LIST

- ☐ _____
- ☐ _____
- ☐ _____
- ☐ _____
- ☐ _____
- ☐ _____
- ☐ _____

PUBLISHING LIST

- ☐ _____
- ☐ _____
- ☐ _____
- ☐ _____
- ☐ _____
- ☐ _____
- ☐ _____

INTRO

_____
_____
_____

IDEAS / INTERVIEW QUESTIONS

_____
_____
_____
_____
_____
_____
_____
_____
_____
_____
_____
_____
_____
_____
_____

SHOW NOTES

_____
_____
_____
_____
_____
_____
_____
_____
_____
_____
_____
_____

OUTRO

_____
_____
_____

Episode Planner

BIO: _____

_____ *Title*

CONTACT: _____

_____

_____

_____

_____

_____

Topic

WEBSITE: _____

_____

_____

_____

_____

_____

_____

SOCIAL MEDIA: _____

_____

_____

_____

_____

_____

Guest

MAIN POINTS / QUESTIONS TO ASK

- _____
- _____
- _____

CALL TO ACTION

_____
_____
_____
_____
_____

Episode Details

TITLE: _____

GUEST: _____

TOPIC: _____

RECORDING DATE: _____

PUBLISHED DATE: _____

EPISODE #: _____

EP LENGTH: _____

RECORDING LIST

- ☐ _____
- ☐ _____
- ☐ _____
- ☐ _____
- ☐ _____
- ☐ _____
- ☐ _____

EDITING LIST

- ☐ _____
- ☐ _____
- ☐ _____
- ☐ _____
- ☐ _____
- ☐ _____
- ☐ _____

PUBLISHING LIST

- ☐ _____
- ☐ _____
- ☐ _____
- ☐ _____
- ☐ _____
- ☐ _____
- ☐ _____

INTRO

_____
_____

IDEAS / INTERVIEW QUESTIONS

_____
_____
_____
_____
_____
_____
_____
_____
_____
_____
_____
_____
_____
_____
_____
_____
_____

SHOW NOTES

_____
_____
_____
_____
_____
_____
_____
_____
_____
_____
_____
_____

OUTRO

_____
_____
_____

Episode Planner

BIO:

_____
_____
_____
_____
_____
_____
_____
_____
_____
_____

_____
Title

Topic

_____
_____
_____

_____
Guest

CONTACT:

_____
_____

WEBSITE:

_____
_____

SOCIAL MEDIA:

_____
_____

MAIN POINTS / QUESTIONS TO ASK

- _____
- _____
- _____

CALL TO ACTION

_____
_____
_____
_____
_____

Episode Details

TITLE: _____ RECORDING DATE: _____

GUEST: _____ PUBLISHED DATE: _____

TOPIC: _____ EPISODE #: _____

_____ EP LENGTH: _____

RECORDING LIST

- ☐ _____
- ☐ _____
- ☐ _____
- ☐ _____
- ☐ _____
- ☐ _____
- ☐ _____

EDITING LIST

- ☐ _____
- ☐ _____
- ☐ _____
- ☐ _____
- ☐ _____
- ☐ _____
- ☐ _____

PUBLISHING LIST

- ☐ _____
- ☐ _____
- ☐ _____
- ☐ _____
- ☐ _____
- ☐ _____
- ☐ _____

INTRO

_____
_____
_____

IDEAS / INTERVIEW QUESTIONS

_____
_____
_____
_____
_____
_____
_____
_____
_____
_____
_____
_____

SHOW NOTES

_____
_____
_____
_____
_____
_____
_____
_____
_____
_____
_____
_____
_____

OUTRO

_____
_____
_____

Episode Planner

BIO:

CONTACT:

Title

WEBSITE:

Topic

SOCIAL MEDIA:

Guest

MAIN POINTS / QUESTIONS TO ASK

- _____
- _____
- _____

CALL TO ACTION

Episode Details

TITLE: _____

GUEST: _____

TOPIC: _____

RECORDING DATE: _____

PUBLISHED DATE: _____

EPISODE #: _____

EP LENGTH: _____

RECORDING LIST

- ☐ _____
- ☐ _____
- ☐ _____
- ☐ _____
- ☐ _____
- ☐ _____
- ☐ _____

EDITING LIST

- ☐ _____
- ☐ _____
- ☐ _____
- ☐ _____
- ☐ _____
- ☐ _____
- ☐ _____

PUBLISHING LIST

- ☐ _____
- ☐ _____
- ☐ _____
- ☐ _____
- ☐ _____
- ☐ _____
- ☐ _____

INTRO

_____
_____
_____

IDEAS / INTERVIEW QUESTIONS

_____
_____
_____
_____
_____
_____
_____
_____
_____
_____
_____
_____
_____
_____
_____

SHOW NOTES

_____
_____
_____
_____
_____
_____
_____
_____
_____
_____
_____
_____

OUTRO

_____
_____
_____

Episode Planner

BIO:

_____

Title

_____
_____
_____
_____
_____
_____
_____
_____
_____
_____
_____

CONTACT:

_____
_____

Topic

_____
_____
_____

WEBSITE:

_____
_____

SOCIAL MEDIA:

_____
_____
_____

Guest

MAIN POINTS / QUESTIONS TO ASK

- _____
- _____
- _____

CALL TO ACTION

_____
_____
_____
_____
_____

Episode Details

TITLE: _____ RECORDING DATE: _____

GUEST: _____ PUBLISHED DATE: _____

TOPIC: _____ EPISODE #: _____

EP LENGTH: _____

RECORDING LIST

- ☐ _____
- ☐ _____
- ☐ _____
- ☐ _____
- ☐ _____
- ☐ _____
- ☐ _____

EDITING LIST

- ☐ _____
- ☐ _____
- ☐ _____
- ☐ _____
- ☐ _____
- ☐ _____
- ☐ _____

PUBLISHING LIST

- ☐ _____
- ☐ _____
- ☐ _____
- ☐ _____
- ☐ _____
- ☐ _____
- ☐ _____

INTRO

_____

_____

_____

IDEAS / INTERVIEW QUESTIONS

_____

_____

_____

_____

_____

_____

_____

_____

_____

_____

_____

_____

_____

_____

_____

_____

SHOW NOTES

_____

_____

_____

_____

_____

_____

_____

_____

_____

_____

_____

_____

OUTRO

_____

_____

_____

Episode Planner

BIO: _____

_____

_____

_____

_____

_____

_____

_____

_____

_____

_____

_____

_____

_____
Title

Topic

_____

_____

_____

_____
Guest

CONTACT:

_____

_____

WEBSITE:

_____

_____

SOCIAL MEDIA:

_____

_____

MAIN POINTS / QUESTIONS TO ASK

- _____
- _____
- _____

CALL TO ACTION

_____

_____

_____

_____

_____

Episode Details

TITLE: _____

GUEST: _____

TOPIC: _____

RECORDING DATE: _____

PUBLISHED DATE: _____

EPISODE #: _____

EP LENGTH: _____

RECORDING LIST

- ☐ _____
- ☐ _____
- ☐ _____
- ☐ _____
- ☐ _____
- ☐ _____
- ☐ _____

EDITING LIST

- ☐ _____
- ☐ _____
- ☐ _____
- ☐ _____
- ☐ _____
- ☐ _____
- ☐ _____

PUBLISHING LIST

- ☐ _____
- ☐ _____
- ☐ _____
- ☐ _____
- ☐ _____
- ☐ _____
- ☐ _____

INTRO

_____

_____

_____

IDEAS / INTERVIEW QUESTIONS

_____

_____

_____

_____

_____

_____

_____

_____

_____

_____

_____

SHOW NOTES

_____

_____

_____

_____

_____

_____

_____

_____

_____

_____

OUTRO

_____

_____

_____

Episode Planner

BIO:

_____

Title

CONTACT:

Topic

WEBSITE:

SOCIAL MEDIA:

Guest

MAIN POINTS / QUESTIONS TO ASK

• _____

• _____

• _____

CALL TO ACTION

Episode Details

TITLE: _____
GUEST: _____
TOPIC: _____

RECORDING DATE: _____
PUBLISHED DATE: _____
EPISODE #: _____
EP LENGTH: _____

RECORDING LIST

- ☐ _____
- ☐ _____
- ☐ _____
- ☐ _____
- ☐ _____
- ☐ _____
- ☐ _____

EDITING LIST

- ☐ _____
- ☐ _____
- ☐ _____
- ☐ _____
- ☐ _____
- ☐ _____
- ☐ _____

PUBLISHING LIST

- ☐ _____
- ☐ _____
- ☐ _____
- ☐ _____
- ☐ _____
- ☐ _____
- ☐ _____

INTRO

_____
_____
_____

IDEAS / INTERVIEW QUESTIONS

_____
_____
_____
_____
_____
_____
_____
_____
_____
_____
_____
_____
_____
_____
_____

SHOW NOTES

_____
_____
_____
_____
_____
_____
_____
_____
_____
_____

OUTRO

_____
_____
_____

JOIN THE MOVEMENT TO SPARK CONVERSATIONS FOR THE KINGDOM!

Spark Media exists to spark conversations for the kingdom and spread the message of hope through podcasting. Our purpose is empower faith-based podcasters to spread Biblical truth. We equip podcasters through live and virtual events, training from industry leaders, a thriving community of fellow podcasters, and consultations designed to bring knowledge, insight, and clarity to the production process.

Spark Conference

The Spark Christian Podcast Conference is the premiere conference for Christian Podcasters. Attendees receive cutting-edge training, access to high profile speakers, and the opportunity to network with others from the podcasting, writing, and speaking industries.

Conference add-ons include literary appointments, headshots, podcast consultations, and graphic design appointments.

Live Events

Spark Collective

The Spark Collective is a private membership community designed to instruct Christian podcasters on the best practices of the industry and the latest advances in podcasting.

This is accomplished through our extensive video and resource library, Mastermind trainings, interviews with industry experts, and the ability to have of one on one consultations with Spark Media founder, Misty Phillip.

Membership

Spark Network

At Spark Media, we believe in the power of podcasting to spread messages of hope to all nations. Our mission is to share Biblically-based messages to people all around the world via podcasts. And, it all starts with a SPARK! The Spark Network is a podcasting platform dedicated to bringing you engaging Faith-based content through various podcast shows.

www.SparkMedia.Ventures

Made in the USA
Middletown, DE
22 August 2024

59018654R00084